The New England Transcendentalists:
Life of the Mind and of the Spirit

edited by Elle

D0283415

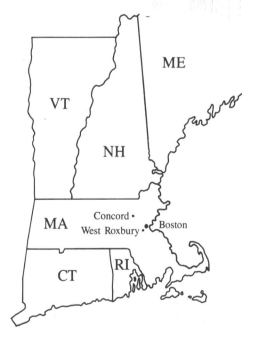

© Discovery Enterprises, Ltd.
Lowell, Massachusetts
1993

© Discovery Enterprises, Ltd., Lowell, MA 1993

ISBN 1-878668-22-6 paperback edition
Library of Congress Catalog Card Number 93-70438

10   9   8   7   6   5   4

Printed in the United States of America

Subject Reference Guide:
Transcendentalists – New England
Brook Farm / Brook Farm School
Henry David Thoreau
Ralph Waldo Emerson
Margaret Fuller
Walt Whitman

Photo Credits
The photographs of Emerson, Thoreau, and the
portrait of Fuller are reprinted with the permission of
the Concord Free Public Library, Concord, Massachusetts.

Illustrations by David K. Deitch of Brook Farm (cover) and
Walt Whitman, are based on interpretations of historic paintings.

Acknowledgments
For their patient, kind assistance in the preparation of
this book, I thank the staffs of the Boston Public Library, the
Concord Free Library, and the Massachusetts Historical Society.

Table of Contents

Dedication

For all those who love to learn and explore;
and especially for Steve,
my lifelong companion in such endeavors.

Foreword

As the Industrial Revolution took hold in New England during the 1830's and 1840's, a small band of people centered in Boston and nearby Concord became alarmed. These people were the New England Transcendentalists. They had a different idea of what "progress" in America should be, and feared that society had more to lose than gain by pursuing a materialistic route. They foresaw that increasing production in the factories meant decreasing the individual's sense of self.

The Transcendentalists began meeting in each other's homes, as well as in favorite bookstores, to exchange ideas. As they developed their philosophies of life, the Transcendentalists started writing books and essays, giving lectures, leading discussions, establishing publications, opening schools, participating in reforms, and planning whole communities based on their beliefs. It was a time of creativity, of studying life from the inside out. The Transcendentalists wanted to understand the life of the mind and of the spirit. They often did this by observing nature closely, and by listening to themselves -- trusting their own thoughts and ideas.

In this book, you'll read the words of many of the Transcendentalists: part of a lecture by Ralph Waldo Emerson, the "spokesman of Transcendentalism;" statements of belief by Henry David Thoreau, perhaps the most famous Transcendentalist; one of the discussions led by Margaret Fuller; and poetry by Walt Whitman. These are called primary sources, because they are the words of the people themselves who lived during that time. Secondary sources are writings based on those primary sources, such as the essay and the historian's account of Emerson's influence, also included here.

Let's start our exploration with the most visible aspect of Transcendentalism: Brook Farm. Brook Farm was the community designed by the Transcendentalists to put their beliefs into practice. The first two readings are the memories of people who, during the 1840's, had been students at the Brook Farm school.

A Girl's Recollections of Brook Farm School

Kate Sloan Gaskill

Overland Monthly, 72 (September 1918): 233-240.

I shall never forget the first impression that Brook Farm and its people made upon me. It was on a Saturday afternoon, early in June, 1843, that my mother, my young brother and I found ourselves at the door of the "Hive," the principal building of the Farm. We had come in the little one-horse bus that ran from Boston to West Roxbury, a distance of nine miles. On the way I had been dreading the entrance into a new life among a people far removed in aims and habits from our kindly neighbors in the little New England village of Weymouth, where much of my life up to this time had been passed.

My mother was full of enthusiasm. She had met and known some of the members of the association and had been touched and impressed by the new doctrine of the so-called "Transcendentalists" that was working like a leaven through all New England life in the late thirties and early forties. My father had recently died and to her, in her loneliness this new home where she was to find brothers and sisters ready to aid her, inspiration for ideals and higher thinking for herself and more than all, broader opportunities for her children, was most welcome. ...

Upon our arrival we were assigned to Pilgrim House, which for three years was to be our home, and here our community life began. The surroundings were very beautiful. The farm was in the center of what has been called "the wild flower garden of New England." It was surrounded by low hills and its meadows and sunny slopes were diversified by the orchard, the quiet groves and the denser pine wood. The latter was called the cathedral and was a favorite place for picnics, pageants and for religious services. Through the green meadow and by the "Hive," near the roadside, ran the brook that gave its name to the farm. No Brook Farmer ever forgot the meadow or the pine grove or the little stream that flowed so musically on its way to join the Charles river. ...

Probably to the present generation a brief review of the purposes and circumstances of the founding of the settlement will not prove uninteresting. The Brook Farm Community or Association, as its members insisted upon calling it, was the natural outgrowth of a spirit of democracy that characterized this period, not only in New England, but in the old world as well, which taught that "Life is finer and more beautiful, kinder and happier where men are devoted to each other's good and where the constant struggle for the means of subsistence is made less urgent and exacting." Probably as early as 1838 the famous "Transcendental Club" of New England had suggested plans for an ideal society where thoughtful and cultivated people should be brought together, where each person should do his share of the manual labor necessary for the physical wants of the community, where all should have time and opportunity for mental culture and where life should be simple and wholesome. George Ripley, Ralph Waldo Emerson, the two famous Channings, uncle and nephew, Nathaniel Hawthorne, Margaret Fuller, James Freeman Clark, Elizabeth Peabody and a score of others met during the winter of 1840 and discussed plans for a practical application of these new views of life. ...

Early in 1841 George Ripley, his wife, and sister, Marianna; Charles A. Dana, Nathaniel Hawthorne and six others, bought a farm of 208 acres at West Roxbury, drew up their articles of association of the subscribers to the Brook Farm Institute of Agriculture and Education, elected their officers and moved out to the one large farmhouse which was already on the place. The farm was to provide subsistence for the members of the association and give an opportunity for that healthy mixture of muscular and mental labor which, it was believed, would be conducive to the highest intellectual achievement. ...

Much work of real value was done at Brook Farm by the men and women who found the surroundings conducive to literary thought and who were inspired by association with kindred minds, but the pride of Brook Farm was in its school. There has never been another such school in America or such teaching as was received by the young people at the Farm. Men and women who were soon to become leaders in the thought and life of the nation gave of their best to the little group of students that came to this wonderful school from all sections of New England, from New York, from Cuba and even from far-off Manila. ...

Upon the afternoon of our arrival the "Hive" was the scene of activity. A dance was to be given that night and all the girls, several of whom were near my own age, (I was just fifteen), were to wear wreaths of wild daisies. ...The girls made a wreath for me and were so cordial and kindly ... I remember thinking that it was strange that I felt so much at home already. ...

Early on Monday morning, after a quiet, restful Sunday, while the older members were engaged in the necessary duties of the farm and household, school work began for the younger people. George Ripley taught Intellectual and moral philosophy and mathematics. His wife, Sophia Willard Ripley, for years before her marriage one of the most famous teachers in Boston, was instructor in modern languages and history. Charles A. Dana had classes in

Greek and German and John S. Dwight imparted a knowledge of music and Latin. There was an instructor in drawing, a lecturer on the theory and practice of agriculture and several teachers for the younger children. Ralph Waldo Emerson, Margaret Fuller, Theodore Parker, Horace Greeley, Bronson Alcott, and indeed, most of the famous men and women of that day came to lecture to us or better still, to talk at their ease in the free, inspiring atmosphere. ...

Like the college boys and girls of today we were in the habit of giving nicknames to our teachers ... Miss Marianna Ripley had charge of the dining room. She was very tall and straight and the mischievous boys and girls spoke of her as "Her Perpendicular Majesty." ...

Every pupil in the school, as well as every member of the association, was expected to devote from one to four hours a day to such manual labor as inclination or natural aptitude suggested, as farming, gardening, care of animals or some form of domestic labor, always under the direction of an instructor. For this work we were paid ten cents an hour and the amount credited to us was deducted from our regular bills. Brook Farm School was, I believe, the first institution in America to place industrial and intellectual training on the same plane. It was a vocational school of an ideal type and did much to impress upon residents and visitors a sense of the real dignity of the humblest necessary task and an appreciation of skill in the performance of the most commonplace duties. The workers were arranged in groups, changing occasionally from one group to another. I was at various times during the three years of my stay at the school in the dormitory group, the mending group, the typesetting group and in the dining room group. I liked the latter group the least, especially on pleasant summer evenings when I wished to go out for a walk in the groves or by the brook.

But our daily life was not given up entirely to study and work. There was an amusement group made up from the instructors and older members, whose business it was to provide entertainment. Dancing parties, picnics, musicals, pageants, plays, rural fetes and tableaux filled up our leisure hours. ...

We often acted characters and proverbs and impromptu dialogues were encouraged by our teachers. The latter frequently gave Shakespearean readings or related the classic myths of Greek and Rome as we sat about the fireplace during a winter's storm. The "Twice Told Tales" were strangely familiar to all Brook Farmers when Nathaniel Hawthorne gave them to a wider audience long after he had left the Farm. ... We had our own newspaper, too, at the Farm -- the Harbinger. ...

Our life was exceedingly simple. In May, 1841, Hawthorne wrote to his sister, "We arise at half past six, dine at half past twelve, and go to bed at nine." This custom prevailed at Brook Farm throughout all its history and was varied only on evenings when dances were given. Then the hour for retiring was ten. The food was plain but wholesome. The favorite breakfast dish was "Brewis" white or brown bread boiled in milk. Meat was served once a day and vegetables were abundant. As many of the residents were vegetarians there was a "graham table" and we young people insisted that better food was served here than at the other tables. During the last year when financial conditions made it necessary to economize we willingly denied ourselves the more expensive foods. We had "meatless days" and butter was rarely served although students who could afford it bought small squares and took them to the table.

During the first year of our residence the women wore a convenient dress when about their work which years later became very popular and was known as "bloomers." For some reason this comfortable working costume was soon given up and we returned to the style prevailing among our neighbors. The men from the beginning discarded the conventional dress coat and wore, on all occasions, a loose tunic about the length of the ordinary coat and confined at the waist with a wide leather belt. Men and women wore wide brimmed hats, the girls frequently decorating their's with wreaths of wild flowers...

[T]he first great misfortune came to Brook Farm in the shape of a small-pox epidemic. ... I was one of the earlier victims. When the doctor decided that a slight cold and fever from which I was suffering were the symptoms of the dreaded disease Mr. Ripley came to Pilgrim House with the carriage, placed me in it and took me to the cottage, walking by the side of the vehicle and talking in the most cheerful manner all the way. I remained there three weeks. Each day my mother made cocoa for me and left it under a tree in front of the cottage. After she had gone I would go out and get it. ...

Spring came early that year and new hope was around. ... [I]t was decided to have a dance at the "Hive" ...[and] it was the gayest crowd that had gathered in months. Everybody was there. ... Louise was at the piano and the floor was filled for the first dance when someone called, "the Phalanstery is on fire!" The dancing stopped and all rushed from the room. The sky was ablaze and the snow-covered ground was red from the reflection. ...

Fire engines came from the surrounding villages and even from Boston, but they were too late to be of any service. The baker had just taken the bread for the next day's breakfast from the oven, and this, with hot coffee, made and served by the boys and men, were given to the tired firemen. Mr. Ripley, determinedly cheerful as usual, made them a little speech. He assured them that they were welcome to the poor hospitality we offered. He asked that they excuse its meagerness on account of the unexpectedness of their visit and assured them that if their hosts had known that they were coming they would have received a worthier, if not a warmer, reception.

When my mother returned the day after the fire she knew the end was near. ... Within a few months after the fire the school closed, Brook Farm was deserted and we turned our faces from the happiest home we had ever known.

A Boy's Recollections of Brook Farm
Arthur Sumner
New England Magazine, 10 (May 1894): 309-313.

Let it be understood, at the outset, that I know very little about the origin or general scope of the famous Brook Farm enterprise. I only present my own life there, so far as I can recall it. I was about sixteen years old at the time. The impressions of my year at Brook Farm remain perfectly distinct in my mind, after a lapse of fifty years. ...

There were many boarders; and most of them were young people, who received instruction from the members, though there was no regular school. I was one of the scholars; and very little did I learn. That was my own fault. I have never regretted my idleness. I was too busy in the fields and by the river to study. Plenty of time for that afterwards.

We Brook-Farmers were exceedingly happy people, and perfectly satisfied with our little isolated circle. ... This famous experiment, since known almost the world over, had a life of seven years. There were a hundred people present during my time; but I cannot remember more than three married couples, though there were several betrothals which afterwards led to marriage.

I don't believe anybody was ever hurt by being at Brook Farm. The life was pure, the company choice. There was a great deal of hard work, and plenty of fun, -- music, dancing, reading, skating, moonlight walks, and some flirting in pairs. After the dispersal, the people went back to the world, and most of them prospered.

Mr. George Ripley was the head man. ... [He] favored our going to church; so they used to rig up a two-horse hay wagon, of a Sunday morning, and ride over to Theodore Parker's meeting-house in West Roxbury, a pretty village two miles away. I think I went once. ...

Mr. John Dwight used to come in from his toil in the hot sun at noon, to give me a lesson on the piano; and after faithfully doing that job, he would lie down on the lounge and go to sleep, while I played to him. What a piece of nonsense it was, to have a man like that hoeing corn and stiffening his fingers! But the idea was (I think) that all kinds of labor must be made equally honorable, and that the poet, painter and philosopher must take their turn at the plough or in the ditch. ...

To me this year of my youthful life stands out single and conspicuous. Simply as a happy memory, it is inestimable. I learned little or nothing from books, and only worked occasionally in the fields, just to amuse myself. But the regular members worked in the house, or out of doors, at general farm work, domestic duties, and in giving lessons to the pupils. The ladies used to go round from house to house, to do the chamber work in the morning; and in rainy weather they were sometimes escorted by us boys, who held our umbrellas over them. The washing and ironing were done at the Pilgrim House, by another "group." There it was that I first learned to iron towels. ...

The Farm had about one hundred acres. Lying in the gently hilly country that stretches southwest of Boston, bordered by primeval forests of pine and dotted with elms and (am I right?) ash trees, with the beautiful river Charles not far away, you can conceive how delightful was the landscape wherever we went; in summer or winter, in the woods or by the river, boating, skating, or walking, there was nothing that was not beautiful. And we were all alone. Except for an occasional farm wagon that rumbled along the quiet country road skirting one side, I never saw any but our own people, though I wandered for miles through the forest and down the river.

I remember a fancy-dress picnic in the woods, which might have furnished Mr. Hawthorne his scene in the "Blithedale Romance." ... Hawthorne lived at Brook Farm in the early days, but I never saw him there. Afterwards I saw him for just one second. It was at the door of Miss Peabody's book room* in West Street. Oh, ye old Bostonians, most blessed of mankind, what happy memories are associated with that famous room, the resort of poets, philosophers, painters, thinkers! Mr. Hawthorne appeared for an instant at the door, and then vanished; but not before I had taken an impression of him, which may be wrong, but is ineffaceable. What I saw, with near-sighted eyes, was a rather tall, youngish, well-made, poetical-looking man, who came to the door and fled away before the crowd. ...

We had a great deal of company, -- curious tourists from abroad, artistic people, and socialists. It became necessary to charge a moderate price for their accommodation. The houses were, first, The Hive, largest and oldest. It was an old farmhouse, standing near the quiet country road, the land sloping down in front to a pretty brook which ran through the farm to join the river. Close by was a magnificent elm. The Hive contained the kitchen and dining-room, and thither flocked the whole Community, summoned three times a day by a bugle horn, which set the black dog a-howling. The other houses were about a quarter of a mile away, and a few hundred yards from each other. One of them was built by Mr. Morton of Plymouth, and was called the Pilgrim House. ... Nearby was a brown house called The Cottage. The first time I slept at

*See Notes pg. 45

the farm I was put into a room in this house, and, the night being cool, I got up and laid a table upside down on the bedspread as a blanket. I do not recommend the expedient, but I slept well that night. Next to the Cottage was The Erie, a square, frail house, standing on some high terraces, and looking over a wide prospect of meadow and hill. Back of it, within a few rods, a pine forest stretched away ...

I must tell who "we boys" were. During my year there were not many. There were two Spanish boys from Manila, who had been consigned by their father to a Boston merchant, to be sent to school; so they were kept at Brook Farm for several years. ... For a little while there was a crowd of Cuban boys ... There might have been a dozen more boys. ...

It was a beautiful idyllic life which we led, with plenty of work and play and transcendentalism ...

Ralph Waldo Emerson never lived at Brook Farm, but he is considered the "spokesman of Transcendentalism" because his books, essays, and lectures inspired so many other Transcendentalists. A section of The American Scholar *lecture he gave in Cambridge follows.*

The American Scholar
A lecture delivered by Ralph Waldo Emerson
August 31, 1837

...The first in time and the first in importance of the
influences upon the mind is that of nature. Every day, the
sun; and, after sunset, Night and her stars. Ever the winds
blow; ever the grass grows. ... The scholar is he of all men
whom this spectacle most engages. He must settle its
value in his mind. What is nature to him? There is never
a beginning, there is never an end, to the inexplicable continuity of this web of God, but always circular power returning into itself. Therein it resembles his own spirit,
whose beginning, whose ending, he never can find, - so
entire, so boundless. ... Nature hastens to render account
of herself to the mind. Classification begins. To the
young mind every thing is individual, stands by itself. By
and by, it finds how to join two things and see in them one
nature; then three, then three thousand; and so, ... it goes
on tying things together, ... discovering roots running under ground whereby contrary and remote things cohere
and flower out from one stem. It presently learns that
since the dawn of history there has been a constant accu-
mulation and classifying of facts. But what is classification but the perceiving that these objects are not chaotic,
and are not foreign, but have a law which is also a law of
the human mind? The astronomer discovers that geome-
try, a pure abstraction of the human mind, is the measure
of planetary motion. The chemist finds proportions and
intelligible method throughout matter; and science is

Ralph Waldo Emerson

nothing but the finding of analogy, identity, in the most remote parts. The ambitious soul sits down before each refractory fact; one after another reduces all strange constitutions, all new powers, to their class and their law, and goes on forever to animate the last fibre of organization, the outskirts of nature, by insight.

Thus to him, to this schoolboy under the bending dome of day, is suggested that he and it proceed from one root; one is leaf and one is flower; relation, sympathy, stirring in every vein. And what is that root? Is not that the soul of his soul? A thought too bold; a dream too wild. Yet when this spiritual light shall have revealed the law of more earthly natures, - when he has learned to worship the soul, ... [h]e shall see that nature is the opposite of the soul, answering to it part for part. One is seal and one is print. Its beauty is the beauty of his own mind. Its laws are the laws of his own mind. Nature then becomes to him the measure of his attainments. So much of nature as he is ignorant of, so much of his own mind does he not yet possess. And, in fine, the ancient precept, "Know thyself," and the modern precept, "Study nature," become at last one maxim. ...

Note: The Transcendentalists' writings in this book have been reprinted as they were first published in the 1800's. Some spellings and expressions may therefore appear archaic.

The Seer

Octavius Brooks Frothingham was one of the first historians to write about the Transcendental movement, publishing his book Transcendentalism in New England *in 1876. He labeled Ralph Waldo Emerson "the seer" (a person who foresees or predicts things), and described Emerson's wide influence in both the United States and Europe. In the section below, Frothingham showed the effect Emerson had on the German writer Herman Grimm.*

... [Grimm] saw a volume of [Emerson's book] "Essays" lying on the table of an American acquaintance, looked into it, and was surprised that, being tolerably well practised in reading English, he understood next to nothing of the contents. He asked about the author, and, learning that he was highly esteemed in his own country, he opened the book again, read further, and was so much struck by passages here and there, that he borrowed it, carried it home, took down Webster's dictionary, and began reading in earnest. ... [T]he unexpected turns of thought, the use of original words, embarrassed him at first; but soon he discovered the secret and felt the charm. The man had fresh thoughts, employed a living speech, was a genuine person. ...

The historian Frothingham then quoted Grimm directly; the following are Grimm's words, describing how he felt reading Emerson.

"As I read, all seems old and familiar as if it was my own well-worn thought; all seems new as if it never occurred to me before. I found myself depending on the book and was provoked with myself for it. How could I be so captured and enthralled; so fascinated and bewitched? The writer was but a man like any other; yet, on taking up the volume again, the spell was renewed -- I felt the pure air; the old weather-beaten motives recovered their tone." ...

"He regards the world in its immediate aspect, with fresh vision; the thing done or occurring before him opens the way to serene heights. The living have precedence of the dead. Even the living of to-day of the Greeks of yesterday, nobly as the latter thought, moulded, chiselled, sang. For me was the breath of life, for me the rapture of spring, for me love and desire, for me the secret of wisdom and power." ...

"Emerson fills me with courage and confidence. He has read and observed, but he betrays no sign of toil. He presents familiar facts, but he places them in new lights and combinations. From every object the lines run straight out, connecting it with the central point of life. What I had hardly dared to think, it was so bold, he brings forth as quietly as if it was the most familiar commonplace. He is a perfect swimmer on the ocean of modern existence. He dreads no tempest, for he is sure that calm will follow it; he does not hate, contradict, or dispute, for he understands men and loves them. I look on with wonder to see how the hurly-burly of modern life subsides, and the elements gently betake themselves to their allotted places. Had I found but a single passage in his writings that was an exception to this rule, I should begin to suspect my judgment, and should say no further word; but long acquaintance confirms my opinion. As I think of this man, I have understood the devotion of pupils who would share any fate with their master, because his genius banished doubt and imparted life to all things."

Emerson's words also inspired his own countrymen, including Henry David Thoreau. Emerson's lectures and his book Nature *first convinced Thoreau to keep a journal and to look to nature as a guide. On July 4, 1845, Thoreau began his famous experiment of leading a simplified life in the woods near Walden Pond. He wrote about that experience in his book* Walden.

Walden
Henry David Thoreau

When I wrote the following pages, or rather the bulk of them, I lived alone, in the woods, a mile from any neighbor, in a house which I had built myself, on the shore of Walden Pond, in Concord, Massachusetts, and earned my living by the labor of my hands only. I lived there two years and two months. At present I am a sojourner in civilized life again. ...

There is some of the same fitness in a man's building his own house that there is in a bird's building its own nest. Who knows but if men constructed their dwellings with their own hands, and provided food for themselves and families simply and honestly enough, the poetic faculty would be universally developed, as birds universally sing when they are so engaged? But alas! we do like cowbirds and cuckoos, which lay their eggs in nests which other birds have built, and cheer no traveller with their chattering and unmusical notes. Shall we forever resign the pleasure of construction to the carpenter? ... Where is this division of labor to end? and what object does it finally serve? No doubt another *may* also think for me; but it is not therefore desirable that he should do so to the exclusion of my thinking for myself. ...

Every morning was a cheerful invitation to make my life of equal simplicity, and I may say innocence, with Nature herself. I have been as sincere a worshipper of Aurora as the Greeks. I got up early and bathed in the pond; that was a religious exercise, and one of the best things which I did. They say that characters were engraven on the bathing tub of [a Chinese] king to this effect: "Renew thyself completely each day; do it again, and again, and forever again." I can understand that. ...

I went to the woods because I wished to live deliberately, to front only the essential facts of life, and see if I could not learn what it had to teach, and not, when I came to die, discover that I had not lived. I did not wish to live what was not life, living is so dear; nor did I wish to practise resignation, unless it was quite necessary. ...

Our life is frittered away by detail. ... Simplify, simplify. Instead of three meals a day, if it be necessary eat but one; instead of a hundred dishes, five; and reduce other things in proportion. ...

I did not read books the first summer; I hoed beans. Nay, I often did better than this. There were times when I could not afford to sacrifice the bloom of the present moment to any work, whether of the head or hands. I love a broad margin to my life. Sometimes, in a summer morning, having taken my accustomed bath, I sat in my sunny doorway from sunrise till noon, ... amidst the pines and hickories and sumachs, in undisturbed solitude and stillness, while the birds sang around or flitted noiseless through the house, until by the sun falling in at my west window, or the noise of some traveller's wagon on the distant highway, I was reminded of the lapse of time. I grew in those seasons like corn in the night, and they were far better than any work of the hands would have been. ...

I had three chairs in my house; one for solitude, two for friendship, three for society. ... I could not but notice some of the peculiarities of my visitors. Girls and boys and young women generally seemed glad to be in the woods. They looked in the pond and at the flowers, and improved their time. Men of business, even farmers,

thought only of solitude and employment, and of the great
distance at which I dwelt from something or other; and
though they said that they loved a ramble in the woods occasionally, it was obvious that they did not. ...

Instead of calling on some scholar, I paid many a visit
to particular trees, of kinds which are rare in this neigh-
borhood, standing far away in the middle of some pasture,
or in the depths of a wood or swamp, or on a hill-top; such
as the black-birch, of which we have some handsome
specimens two feet in diameter; its cousin the yellow-birch
... or a more perfect hemlock than usual, standing like a
pagoda in the midst of the woods; and many others I could
mention. These were the shrines I visited both summer
and winter. ...

I left the woods for as good a reason as I went there.
Perhaps it seemed to me that I had several more lives to
live, and could not spare any more time for that one. It is
remarkable how easily and insensibly we fall into a particular route, and make a beaten track for ourselves. I had
not lived there a week before my feet wore a path from my
door to the pond-side ... The surface of the earth is soft
and impressible by the feet of men; and so with the paths
which the mind travels. How worn and dusty, then, must
be the highways of the world, how deep the ruts of tradi-
tion and conformity! ...

I learned this, at least, by my experiment; that if one
advances confidently in the direction of his dreams, and
endeavors to live the life which he has imagined, he will
meet with a success unexpected in common hours. He
will put some things behind, will pass an invisible bound-
ary; new, universal, and more liberal laws will begin to
establish themselves around and within him; or the old
laws be expanded, and interpreted in his favor in a more
liberal sense, and he will live with the license of a higher

order of beings. In proportion as he simplifies his life, the laws of the universe will appear less complex, and solitude will not be solitude, nor poverty poverty, nor weakness weakness. If you have built castles in the air, your work need not be lost; that is where they should be. Now put the foundations under them. ...

Building a New Philosophy of Life

The Transcendentalists liked sharing their ideas in conversation as well as in writing. In fact, that's how it all began.

As early as 1836, a group of people (later known as "the Transcendental Club") met in George Ripley's study in Boston to explore ideas together. The regulars in this group, which met four or five times a year until the early 1840's, included George and Sophia Ripley, Ralph Waldo Emerson, Bronson Alcott, Margaret Fuller, Elizabeth Peabody, Henry Thoreau, John Dwight, Theodore Parker, Jones Very, Frederic Hedge, James Clarke and Convers Francis, among others. Most of the men were Harvard graduates and had been trained as Unitarian ministers, which led them to discuss religious subjects at first. They were not happy with Unitarianism,* feeling it lacked a positive approach to life and religion, so they began to explore a new kind of faith.

Other members, particularly Margaret Fuller and Bronson Alcott, believed that society's progress depended on the improvement of its individual members. They expressed strong ideas about education.

These discussions grew into plans for action and reform. As we've seen, one of the most famous plans they developed was for the Brook Farm community. Even Transcendentalists who never lived at Brook Farm (Fuller, Emerson ...) helped define and plan the community, and later served as guest instructors at its school.

Bronson Alcott* introduced the discussion method of teaching at his Temple School in Boston during the 1830's.

*See Notes pg. 45

28

Margaret Fuller

He started a series of "Conversations on the Gospels," encouraging his young students to use their natural intuition to discover the meaning of passages in the Bible. Elizabeth Peabody and Margaret Fuller assisted Alcott in running his school in this open fashion.

Margaret Fuller soon began her own series of discussions. These weekly "Conversations" were held at Elizabeth Peabody's bookstore and continued for four years. At 11 o'clock on Saturday mornings, twenty-five to forty women would gather to share their ideas on the topic of the day. They often discussed themes represented in Greek mythology (will, understanding, reason, love ...) or general topics like "Education" or "the Fine Arts." Fuller chose topics broad enough to encourage all to participate.

By this time, Elizabeth Peabody's bookstore had become a kind of haven for the Transcendentalists; it was their informal meeting place in the city. Her bookstore carried foreign books and periodicals, and many of the Transcendentalists were reading works by such European writers and philosophers as Kant, Goethe, and Coleridge. The Transcendentalists could be sure of meeting someone they knew there; and soon they started holding meetings at the bookstore. Peabody went on to become the first woman publisher in Boston, and, probably, in the nation.

Ralph Waldo Emerson continued challenging audiences, through his writings and lectures, to think differently about life. Don't simply be an economic piece in society's plan, he urged them, try to become whole beings again. Self-reliance! Individuality! Study nature to know yourself!

"People wish to be settled," Emerson said, but "only as far as they are unsettled is there any hope for them." The only securities are "life, transition, the energizing spirit." Emerson pushed people to learn and grow and change, to think for themselves.

When publications such as the Unitarian's *Christian Examiner* refused to publish their "radical" writings, the Transcendentalists turned to starting their own publications. *The Dial*, a quarterly "Magazine for Literature,

Philosophy and Religion," was perhaps the most famous Transcendental journal. Its first issue was published on July 1, 1840, and, edited by Fuller and Emerson, the publication ran for four years. *The Dial* published the Transcendentalists' poetry, essays (including "The Great Lawsuit"*), book reviews, articles on reforms here in the United States and abroad, philosophical discussions, and religious debates.

Other Transcendental publications included *The Western Messenger, Boston Quarterly Review, The Present,* Brook Farm's *Harbinger, The Massachusetts Quarterly Review, Aesthetic Papers,* and *Spirit of the Age.* Many of these publications lasted no more than a few years. Interestingly, *Aesthetic Papers* failed after only a single issue, yet that issue contained one of the most famous essays ever written: Henry Thoreau's "Resistance to Civil Government" (later retitled "Civil Disobedience").

The Transcendentalists were seekers. They searched for intellectual and spiritual truth. Some, like Thoreau, looked for answers in the facts of nature; others, like Emerson, dealt with principles. Many Transcendentalists, including Emerson, Thoreau and Fuller, recorded their ongoing search for a new philosophy of life in journals or diaries. Emerson wrote of exchanging private journals with Fuller and Alcott: reading the inner thoughts of the other, taking notes on them, writing comments to them. The Transcendentalists also met in each other's homes, particularly in the study of Emerson's Concord home, to discuss their current ideas. Others, such as Theodore Parker, stayed on as ministers, writing and preaching their views from the pulpit.

The Transcendentalists enjoyed reading, thinking, writing, and perhaps most of all, discussing their ideas.

*See Notes pg. 45

But they also felt strongly about putting their beliefs into action. Beyond the communities and schools they founded, the Transcendentalists were active in all the major reforms of their day: movements to abolish slavery, reform religion, gain rights for women, reform education, and improve conditions for the poor, the insane, and the criminal.

What is Transcendentalism? "Idealism as it appears in 1842," replied Emerson in a lecture that year. One hundred fifty years later, we might add that it is a philosophy of life, learning, and reform that has inspired each new generation of Americans.

The next reading is a section from the Conversation on "What is Life," led by Margaret Fuller.

A Transcendental Conversation*

March 22, 1841. The question of the day was, "What is Life?"

"Let us define, each in turn, our idea of living." Margaret did not believe that we had, any of us, a distinct idea of life.

A[nna] S[haw] thought so great a question ought to be given for a written definition. "No," said Margaret, "that is of no use. When we go away to think of anything, we never do think. We all talk of life. We all have some thought now. Let us tell it. C[aroline Sturgis], what is life?"

Caroline replied, "It is to laugh, or cry ..."

"Good," said Margaret, "but not grave enough. Come, what is life? I know what I think; I want you to find out what you think." ...

Mrs. E[merson]: "We live by the will of God, and the object of life is to submit," and went on into Calvinism.* ...

Mrs. H[ooper] said, "God created us in order to have a perfect sympathy from us as free beings."

Mrs. A[lmira] B[arlow] said she thought the object of life was to attain absolute freedom. At this Margaret immediately and visibly kindled.

C[aroline] S[turgis] said, "God creates from the fullness of life, ... he created us to overflow, ... creation is his happiness and ours."

Margaret was then pressed to say what she considered life to be.

*See Notes pg. 46

Her answer was so full, clear, and concise, ... here are some fragments of her satisfying statement.

She began with God as Spirit, Life, so full as to create and love eternally, yet capable of pause. Love and creativeness are dynamic forces, out of which we, individually, as creatures, go forth bearing his image; that is, having within our being the same dynamic forces by which we also add constantly to the total sum of existence, and shaking off ignorance, and its effects, and by becoming more ourselves, *i.e.*, more divine - destroying sin in its principle, we attain to absolute freedom, we return to God, conscious like himself, and, as his friends, giving, as well as receiving, felicity forevermore. In short, we become gods, and able to give the life which we now feel ourselves able only to receive. ...

Civil Disobedience
Henry David Thoreau

In 1846, Thoreau was locked up in the Concord jail overnight for refusing to pay his poll tax (he hadn't paid in several years). He was released the next day because a relative paid the tax. But he'd made his point: he could not pay taxes to an unjust government - one that allowed slavery and that waged war against Mexico simply to acquire more territory. Thoreau prepared a lecture to explain his actions, which was then published as an essay in 1849.

That essay, Civil Disobedience, *became a classic by the end of the century. It has been called the "Declaration of Independence for the Conscience." Thoreau's belief in using nonviolent but complete resistance to unjust authority has deeply influenced many people, including: Leo Tolstoy (Russian author and philosopher); Mahatma Gandhi (Indian nationalist leader, whose life and work centered on nonviolent noncooperation); and Martin Luther King, Jr. (American civil rights leader).*

I heartily accept the motto, -- "That government is best which governs least;" ... Carried out, it finally amounts to this, which also I believe, -- "That government is best which governs not at all;" and when men are prepared for it, that will be the kind of government which they will have. ...

Can there not be a government in which majorities do not virtually decide right and wrong, but conscience? ... Must the citizen ever for a moment, or in the least degree, resign his conscience to the legislator? Why has every man a conscience, then? I think that we should be men first, and subjects afterward. It is not desirable to cultivate a respect for the law, so much as for the right. The only obligation which I have a right to assume is to do at any time what I think right. ... Law never made men a whit more just; and, by means of their respect for it, even the well-disposed are daily made the agents of injustice. A common and natural result of an undue respect for law is, that you may see a file of soldiers, ... marching in admirable order over hill and dale to the wars, against their wills, ay, against their common sense and consciences, ... they are all peaceably inclined. Now, what are they? Men at all? or small movable forts ...

The mass of men serve the state thus, not as men mainly, but as machines, with their bodies. ... In most cases there is no free exercise whatever of the judgment or of the moral sense; but they put themselves on a level with wood and earth and stones; and wooden men can perhaps be manufactured that will serve the purpose as well. ... Yet such as these even are commonly esteemed good citizens. ... Others -- as most legislators, politicians, lawyers, ministers, and office-holders -- serve the state chiefly with their heads; and, as they rarely make any moral distinctions, they are as likely to serve the Devil, without *intending* it, as God. A very few, as heroes, patriots, martyrs, reformers in the great sense, and *men*, serve the state with their consciences also, and so necessarily resist it for the most part; and they are commonly treated as enemies by it. ...

How does it become a man to behave toward this American government to-day? I answer, that he cannot without disgrace be associated with it. I cannot for an instant recognize that political organization as *my* government which is the *slave's* government also. ...

Henry David Thoreau

It is not so important that many should be as good as you, as that there be some absolute goodness somewhere; for that will leaven the whole lump. There are thousands who are *in opinion* opposed to slavery and to the war [with Mexico], who yet in effect do nothing to put an end to them ...

Unjust laws exist: shall we be content to obey them, or shall we endeavor to amend them, and obey them until we have succeeded, or shall we transgress them at once? Men generally, under such a government as this, think that they ought to wait until they have persuaded the majority to alter them. They think that, if they should resist, the remedy would be worse than the evil. ...

I know this well, that if one thousand, if one hundred, if ten men whom I could name, -- if ten *honest* men only, -- ay, if *one* HONEST man, in this State of Massachusetts, *ceasing to hold slaves*, were actually to withdraw from this copartnership, and be locked up in the county jail therefor, it would be the abolition of slavery in America. For it matters not how small the beginning may seem to be: what is once well done is done forever. But we love better to talk about it ...

Under a government which imprisons any unjustly, the true place for a just man is also a prison. ... If the alternative is to keep all just men in prison, or give up war and slavery, the State will not hesitate which to choose. If a thousand men were not to pay their tax-bills this year, that would not be a violent and bloody measure, as it would be to pay them, and enable the State to commit violence and shed innocent blood. This is, in fact, the definition of a peaceable revolution, if any such is possible. ... But even suppose blood should flow. Is there not a sort of blood shed when the conscience is wounded? Through this would a man's real manhood and immortality flow out, and he bleeds to an everlasting death. I see this blood flowing now. ...

I have paid no poll-tax for six years. I was put into a jail once on this account, for one night; and, as I stood considering the walls of solid stone, two or three feet thick, the door of wood and iron, a foot thick, and the iron

grating which strained the light, I could not help being
struck with the foolishness of that institution which treated
me as if I were mere flesh and blood and bones, to be
locked up. I wondered that it should have concluded at
length that this was the best use it could put me to, and had
never thought to avail itself of my services in some way. I
saw that, if there was a wall of stone between me and my
townsmen, there was a still more difficult one to climb or
break through before they could get to be as free as I was.
I did not for a moment feel confined, and the walls seemed
a great waste of stone and mortar. I felt as if I alone of all
my townsmen had paid my tax. ... I could not but smile to
see how industriously they locked the door on my medita-
tions, which followed them out again without let or hin-
drance, and *they* were really all that was dangerous. As
they could not reach me, they had resolved to punish my
body; just as boys, if they cannot come at some person
against whom they have a spite, will abuse his dog. I saw
that the State ... did not know its friends from its foes, and
I lost all my remaining respect for it, and pitied it.

Thus the State never intentionally confronts a man's
sense, intellectual or moral, but only his body, his senses.
It is not armed with superior wit or honesty, but with superior physical strength. I was not born to be forced. I
will breathe after my own fashion. Let us see who is the
strongest. What force has a multitude? They only can
force me who obey a higher law than I. They force me to
become like themselves. I do not hear of *men* being *forced*
to live this way or that by masses of men. What sort of
life were that to live? When I meet a government which
says to me, "Your money or your life," why should I be in
haste to give it my money? It may be in a great strait, and
not know what to do: I cannot help that. It must help itself; do as I do. ... I perceive that, when an acorn and a

chestnut fall side by side, the one does not remain inert to make way for the other, but both obey their own laws, and spring and grow and flourish as best they can, till one, perchance, overshadows and destroys the other. If a plant cannot live according to its nature, it dies; and so a man. ...

I do not wish to quarrel with any man or nation. I do not wish to split hairs, to make fine distinctions, or set myself up as better than my neighbors. I seek rather, I may say, even an excuse for conforming to the laws of the land. I am but too ready to conform to them. Indeed, I have reason to suspect myself on this head; and each year, as the tax-gatherer comes round, I find myself disposed to review the acts and position of the general and State governments, and the spirit of the people, to discover a pretext for conformity. ...

The authority of government, even such as I am willing to submit to, -- for I will cheerfully obey those who know and can do better than I, and in many things even those who neither know nor can do so well, -- is still an impure one ... There will never be a really free and enlightened State until the State comes to recognize the individual as a higher and independent power, from which all its own power and authority are derived, and treats him accordingly. I please myself with imagining a State at last which can afford to be just to all men, and to treat the individual with respect as a neighbor; ... [that] would prepare the way for a still more perfect and glorious State, which also I have imagined, but not yet anywhere seen.

Leaves of Grass
Walt Whitman

Walt Whitman

Poet Walt Whitman was greatly influenced by Emerson and the transcendental theory of language. That theory held that (1) words are symbols of things in nature, and (2) nature itself is only a symbol -- of a spiritual reality beyond the world of the senses.

During his lifetime, Whitman published not one, but nine books of poetry bearing the title Leaves of Grass. Leaves of Grass was a language experiment: the different editions used many of the same poems (in revised form) as well as new ones. Here are a few of Whitman's poems.

Miracles.

Why, who makes much of a miracle?
As to me I know of nothing else but miracles,
Whether I walk the streets of Manhattan,
Or dart my sight over the roofs of houses toward the sky,
Or wade with naked feet along the beach just in the edge of the
    water,
Or stand under trees in the woods,
Or talk by day with any one I love, or sleep in the bed at night
       with any one I love,
Or sit at table at dinner with the rest,
Or look at strangers opposite me riding in the car,
Or watch honey-bees busy around the hive of a summer
       forenoon,
Or animals feeding in the fields,
Or birds, or the wonderfulness of insects in the air,
Or the wonderfulness of the sundown, or of stars shining so quiet
       and bright,
Or the exquisite delicate thin curve of the new moon in spring;
These with the rest, one and all, are to me miracles,
The whole referring, yet each distinct and in its place.

To me every hour of the light and dark is a miracle,
Every cubic inch of space is a miracle,
Every square yard of the surface of the earth is spread with
       the same,
Every foot of the interior swarms with the same.

To me the sea is a continual miracle,
The fishes that swim -- the rocks -- the motion of the waves --
       the ships with men in them,
What stranger miracles are there?

No. 39

Sometimes with one I love I fill myself with rage for fear I effuse
      unreturn'd love,
But now I think there is no unreturn'd love, the pay is certain one
      way or another,
Doubtless I could not have perceived the universe,
      or written one of my poems, if I had not freely
      given myself to comrades, to love.

Perfections.

Only themselves understand themselves and the like of
      themselves,
As souls only understand souls.

Definitions

animate - to give life to, fill with life

attainment - accomplishment

Aurora - in mythology, the goddess of the dawn

cohere - to cause to form a united or orderly whole

consign - to give over to the care of another

continuity - an uninterrupted, unbroken course

daguerreotype - an early photograph produced
   on a silver or a silver-covered copper plate

effuse - to pour or spread out

esteem - to regard with respect

felicity - great happiness

fete - an outdoor festival or feast

ineffaceable - can't be erased

inestimable - can't be estimated

inexplicable - can't be explained or interpreted

intelligible - capable of being understood

maxim - a saying

pagoda - a religious building of the Far East

precept - a rule or principle establishing a particular
   standard of action

refractory - unmanageable

render - to make, to express

rod - a unit of length equal to five and a half yards

sojourner - someone who stays in a place temporarily

tableaux - a scene presented on stage by costumed actors
   who remain silent and motionless as if in a picture

Notes

Miss Peabody's book room (p.16): Elizabeth Peabody opened her bookstore on Boston's West Street in 1840, and it soon became the gathering place for the Transcendentalists. Margaret Fuller conducted her famous Conversations here. Discussions which helped shape *the Dial* (the Transcendental publication) and Brook Farm also took place here.

Unitarianism (p.28): the religion from which many of the New England Transcendentalists came. Unitarianism allowed more freedom and tolerance in religious belief than other religions of that time. Even so, many Unitarians dismissed the Transcendentalists as too radical.

Bronson Alcott (p.28): In 1843, a few years after his Temple School closed, Bronson Alcott founded the Fruitlands community in Harvard, Mass. Like Brook Farm, Fruitlands was an experiment in communal living. The Fruitlands community never quite took hold, and lasted only 7 months.

"The Great Lawsuit" (p.31): This essay by Margaret Fuller was based on the idea that all souls are equal, both in heaven and here on earth. Fuller later expanded this essay into her book *Woman in the Nineteenth Century*, a classic of American feminism which directly influenced the 1848 Seneca Falls conference on women's rights.

Transcendental Conversation (p.33): A transcript of the Conversation Margaret Fuller led on March 22, 1841 was included in Fuller's *Memoirs*, prepared by Ralph Waldo Emerson, James Freeman Clarke and William Henry Channing in 1852.

Calvinism (p.33): a strict set of religious beliefs, begun by John Calvin in the 1500s, emphasizing an all-powerful God and salvation of the elect by God's grace alone.

A Selected Bibliography

Anderson, Charles R., ed. *Thoreau's Vision: The Major Essays*. Englewood Cliffs, New Jersey: Prentice-Hall, Inc., 1973.

Blanchard, Paula. *Margaret Fuller: From Transcendentalism to Revolution*. New York: Addison-Wesley Publishing Co., Inc., 1987.

Blodgett, Harold and Bradley, Sculley, ed. *Leaves of Grass*. New York: W.W. Norton & Co., Inc., 1968.

Buell, Lawrence. *Literary Transcendentalism: Style and Vision in the American Renaissance*. Ithaca and London: Cornell University Press, 1973.

Codman, John Thomas. *Brook Farm, Historic and Personal Memoirs*. New York: AMS Press, 1971 (first published in Boston: Arena Publishing Co., 1894).

Ericson, Edward L., ed. *Emerson on Transcendentalism*. New York: Ungar Publishing Co., 1986.

Frothingham, Octavius Brooks. *Transcendentalism in New England*. Gloucester, Mass.: Peter Smith, 1965 (first published in New York: G. P. Putnam's Sons, 1876).

Koster, Donald N. *Transcendentalism in America*. Boston, Mass.: G.K. Hall & Co., 1975.

Miller, Perry, ed. *The American Transcendentalists: Their Prose and Poetry*. Garden City, New York: Doubleday & Co., Inc., 1957.

Myerson, Joel. ed. *The Brook Farm Book: A Collection of First-Hand Accounts of the Community*. New York & London: Garland Publishing, Inc., 1987.

Myerson, Joel, ed. *The Transcendentalists: A Review of Research and Criticism.* New York: The Modern Language Association of America, 1984.

Parsons, Thornton and Simon, Myron, ed. *Transcendentalism and Its Legacy.* Ann Arbor, Michigan: University of Michigan Press, 1967.

Perry, Bliss, ed. *The Heart of Emerson's Journals.* Boston and New York: Houghton Mifflin Co., 1926.

Rose, Anne C. *Transcendentalism as a Social Movement, 1830 - 1850.* New Haven and London: Yale University Press, 1981.

Thomas, Owen, ed. *Henry David Thoreau: Walden and Civil Disobedience.* New York: W.W. Norton & Co., Inc., 1966.

Manuscripts

The major manuscript collections of work by the Transcendentalists are at the Houghton Library (Harvard University), Boston Public Library, Massachusetts Historical Society, Concord Free Public Library, New York Public Library, Henry E. Huntington Library (San Marino, Cal.), Andover-Harvard Theological Library, and Fruitlands Museums (Harvard, Mass.).

Further Reading for Students

Includes Primary Sources:

Adams, J. Donald, ed. *Poems of Ralph Waldo Emerson.* New York: Thomas Y. Crowell Co., 1965.

Allen, Francis. H., ed. *Men of Concord* (from Thoreau's journal, illustrations by N. C. Wyeth). Boston: Houghton Mifflin Co., 1936.

Emerson, Ralph Waldo. *The Sound of Trumpets - Selections from Ralph Waldo Emerson* (illustrations by James Daugherty). New York: The Viking Press, 1971.

Glick, Wendell, ed. *Great Short Works of Henry David Thoreau.* New York: Harper & Row, 1982.

Thoreau, Henry David. *Walden* (a retelling: text selections by Steve Lowe; illustrations by Robert Sabuda). New York: Philomel Books, 1990.

Whitman, Walt. *Voyages - Poems by Walt Whitman* (selected by Lee Bennett Hopkins, illustrations by Charles Mikolaycak). San Diego and New York: Harcourt Brace Jovanovich, 1988.

Secondary Sources:

Derleth, August. *Concord Rebel: A Life of Henry David Thoreau.* Philadelphia and New York: Chilton Book Co., 1962.

Emerson, Edward Waldo. *Henry Thoreau - As Remembered by a Young Friend.* Boston and New York: Houghton Mifflin Co., 1917.

Stoutenburg, Adrien and Baker, Laura Nelson. *Listen America - A Life of Walt Whitman.* New York: Charles Scribner's Sons, 1968.

Wilson, Ellen. *Margaret Fuller: Bluestocking, Romantic, Revolutionary.* New York: Farrar, Straus and Giroux, 1977.

Wood, James Playsted. *The People of Concord.* New York: The Seabury Press, 1970.

Wood, James Playsted. *Trust Thyself: A Life of Ralph Waldo Emerson for the Young Reader.* New York: Pantheon Books, 1964.

About the Author

Ellen Hansen has a B.A. in Languages and Political Science from Middlebury College and a J.D. from American University Law School. After practicing law for a number of years, she taught German and English in Japan for three years. Since returning, she has worked as a freelance writer, writing essays and articles on education for the Boston Sunday Globe, The Boston Business Journal, the Christian Science Monitor, and other publications.

Her goal is to keep learning, every day, and then to find creative ways to share what she's learned. (If she'd lived 150 years ago, surely she'd have been a Transcendentalist.) Recently, her volunteer activities have included serving as a language tutor in Boston's Chinatown, and as a mentor in the Mayor's Youth Leadership Corps, a citywide program in leadership for Boston teenagers.

Ms. Hansen lives with her husband in Boston.

The Perspectives on History Series

Order Form

Ship to:

Name: _____

Address: _____

City: _____ State: _____ Zip: _____

Phone: _____ P.O. Number (if applicable): _____

ISBN (last 3 digits)	Title	Qty	Total
		Sub Total	
		Shipping/Handling	
		Total	

Please add $1.50 per book shipping/handling or $5.00 for any orders over $19.00.